MONTEREY'S MOTHER LODE

by
Randall A. Reinstedt

cover and
map illustrations by
Antone A. Hrusa

D1616247

Copyright © 1977 by Randall A. Reinstedt

If bookstores in your area do not carry "MONTEREY'S MOTHER LODE", copies may be obtained by writing to...

GHOST TOWN PUBLICATIONS

P.O. Drawer 5998
Carmel, CA 93921

Other books by Randall A. Reinstedt, offered by Ghost Town Publications, are:

"GHOSTS, BANDITS AND LEGENDS of old Monterey"
"SHIPWRECKS AND SEA MONSTERS of California's Central Coast"
"TALES, TREASURES AND PIRATES of old Monterey"
"GHOSTLY TALES AND MYSTERIOUS HAPPENINGS of old Monterey"
"WHERE HAVE ALL THE SARDINES GONE?"
"MYSTERIOUS SEA MONSTERS of California's Central Coast"
"INCREDIBLE GHOSTS of old Monterey's HOTEL DEL MONTE"
"INCREDIBLE GHOSTS of the BIG SUR COAST"

Fifth Printing

Published in 1973 as:
GOLD IN THE SANTA LUCIAS

ISBN # 0-933818-01-7
Library of Congress # 79-110351

INTRODUCTION

Beginning with James Wilson Marshall's historic discovery in 1848, the dream of untold riches has played an important part in shaping the history of our thirty-first state. However, as strange as it may seem, Marshall's history-making discovery was not the first gold to be found in this land of plenty.

Tales of "yellow sand" and "golden pebbles", spread by neophytes of California's mission period, predate Marshall's discovery by more than half a century. Unfortunately, the majority of these tales are looked upon by historians as nothing more than colorful legends from a colorful time. Whether the majority of these fascinating tales were based on fact, or were merely fancied dreams of past generations, may never be known. However, word of an 1842 gold strike in southern California's San Feliciano Canyon (of the San Fernando Valley) had much more than dreams to back it up. Over $8,000 worth of gold was taken from this California canyon before the shallow pockets of this forgotten strike were stripped of their wealth.

Talk of gold in the Santa Lucia Mountains to the north also circulated throughout California long before Marshall's 1848 find. Not only were tales of "gold for the taking" spread by mission Indians (and perhaps more than one padre), but a second tale, credited to a wandering Scotsman in the long-ago year of 1833, told of finding flakes of gold in this coastal wilderness.

It is the story of gold in these rugged Pacific peaks that this book is about. Located in the southern portion of California's famed Monterey County lies the little-known — but extremely colorful — Los Burros Mining District. With a documented history of gold in this south county area dating back to the 1850s, the story of this remote mining district is an interesting chapter in the overall history of the Golden State.

3

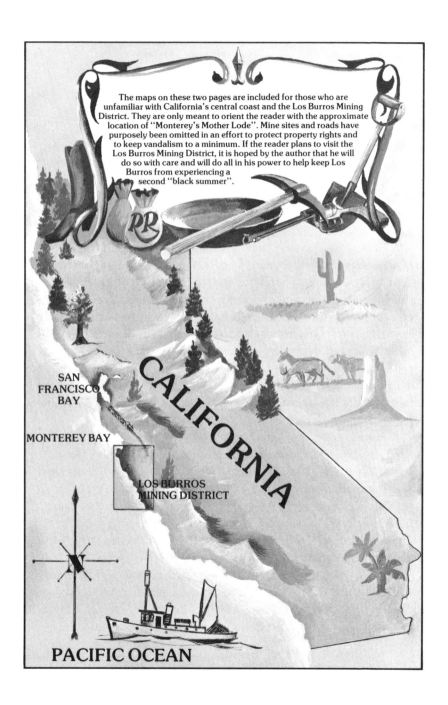

The maps on these two pages are included for those who are unfamiliar with California's central coast and the Los Burros Mining District. They are only meant to orient the reader with the approximate location of "Monterey's Mother Lode". Mine sites and roads have purposely been omitted in an effort to protect property rights and to keep vandalism to a minimum. If the reader plans to visit the Los Burros Mining District, it is hoped by the author that he will do so with care and will do all in his power to help keep Los Burros from experiencing a second "black summer".

SAN
FRANCISCO
BAY

MONTEREY BAY

CALIFORNIA

LOS BURROS
MINING DISTRICT

PACIFIC OCEAN

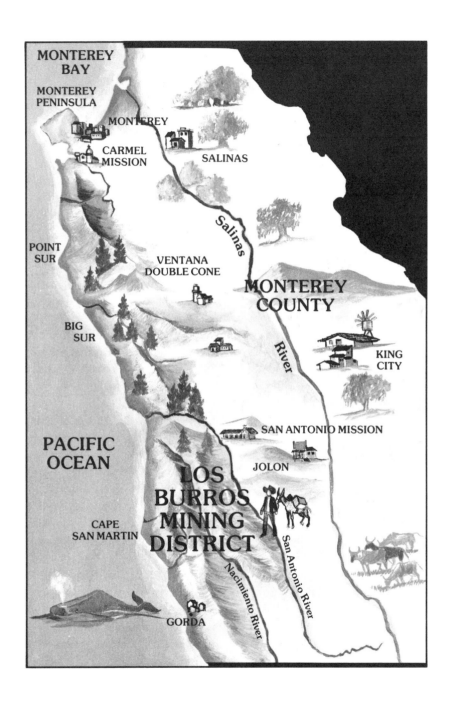

MONTEREY
BAY

MONTEREY
PENINSULA

MONTEREY

CARMEL
MISSION

SALINAS

Salinas

POINT
SUR

VENTANA
DOUBLE CONE

MONTEREY
COUNTY

River

KING
CITY

BIG
SUR

SAN ANTONIO MISSION

JOLON

PACIFIC
OCEAN

LOS
BURROS
MINING
DISTRICT

CAPE
SAN MARTIN

GORDA

Nacimiento River

San Antonio River

ACKNOWLEDGEMENTS

Over the years considerable time has been spent and countless miles have been covered in tracking down and interviewing pioneer descendants and past residents of Monterey County's remote Los Burros Mining District. Without the help and cooperation of these Pacific pioneers, this book could not have been written. Equally as important as the information they gave are the photographs they contributed in their efforts to help make MONTEREY'S MOTHER LODE a reliable and accurate record of gold in the Santa Lucias.

As appropriate as it seems, Charles Krenkel and Adrian Harbolt, two of the gentlemen who contributed a wealth of information as well as valuable photographs, boast surnames of true Los Burros pioneers. These names, as the reader of this book will discover, are deeply woven into the history of the Los Burros Mining District.

Numerous other Monterey County residents and Los Burros veterans such as Howard Krenkel, Ed Plaskett, Homer Stephens, Howard Hilton, Ed Melville, Ken Melville, Harry Downie, Myrtle Leaman, George Heinsen and Jessie Sandholdt should also be acknowledged for their contributions and help.

A special thanks should also be extended to John L. Crisan Jr. for the information and pictures he contributed concerning Monterey County's mysterious cave of death.

Add to this list the names of numerous other old-timers, several dedicated research librarians, countless volumes of California history, early records of California mines and mining districts, and an aged assortment of forgotten newspapers..., and one can only begin to comprehend the number of people and resources that were consulted in the preparation of this work.

Without the cooperation of these individuals and their assistance in locating seldom-used records, it would have been impossible to bring to life the golden years of Los Burros.

Above all, the author wishes to thank his wife Debbie, and his son Erick, for their continued support in helping this book to become a reality.

MONTEREY'S MOTHER LODE

ales of "gold for the taking" have excited settlers of the historic Monterey Peninsula for over two centuries. Tantalizing legends of "yellow sand" and "golden pebbles", spread by neophytes of Father Junipero Serra's Monterey mission, created excitement among the Spanish conquistadores as early as 1770.

With the moving of Mission San Carlos from its original location near the Presidio of Monterey to the mouth of fertile Carmel Valley in June of 1771, Padre Serra insured success for his beloved church, but did little to quiet the stories of the inhabitants of the land.

One such tale boasts a secret mine hidden deep in the Santa Lucias and filled with precious nuggets of gold. Over the years this mysterious cave has become known as the Lost Ventana Mine, and its site has been the object of several treasure-seeking expeditions.

Early Monterey legend tells how Indian braves, at the urging of the Spanish, would strike out from the mission and head for the distant heart of the rugged Santa Lucia Mountains. Continuing in a southerly direction, their path took them across jagged ridges and through rocky canyons, eventually leading to a towering, almost inaccessible peak. This Santa Lucia landmark lies twenty-one air miles from the mission and is known today as Ventana Double Cone. Ventana, Spanish for "window", fits nicely into the tale, as from the summit of this lofty peak the Indians were said to have seen both the bell tower of Carmel Mission and the distant mountain that contained their nugget-filled cave. (In a southerly direction — between the mission and the mountains — Ventana Double Cone is the highest peak of the Santa Lucia Range.)

Continuing south, a day's walk brought the Indians to a secret cave where, legend states, "pebbles of gold lay scattered in a deep underground shaft".

Perhaps this tale of Indian riches is what originally prompted the quest for gold in Monterey's rugged Santa Lucia Mountains. Perhaps the tales of these first Americans were all that was needed to lure the early settlers into these remote Pacific peaks.

Possibly, with the "lost window" of the Lucias escaping detection of these long-ago Spanish prospectors, the ring of picks striking rocks and the footsteps of gold-seekers wandering the Santa Lucia trails were not heard again until the year 1833. In that year, Scottish botanist David Douglas (remembered today for his discovery of the Douglas Fir) reportedly created renewed interest in a possible Monterey mother lode when he wrote from his Peninsula lodgings of finding flakes of gold in the roots of a great tree. This incident, recorded fifteen years before James Wilson Marshall's cry of gold echoed throughout the western world, was perhaps the first actual glimpse of the Santa Lucia's hidden wealth seen by an "outsider". (It should be noted here that even though Douglas is sometimes given credit for having discovered gold in the Santa Lucias, unconfirmed reports point to a Spaniard, Father Luis Antonio Martinez of San Luis Obispo Mission, as having taken gold from the Coast Range long before Douglas tramped the Santa Lucia wilderness.)

Mining records do not record organized activity in the Santa Lucia Mountains until the early 1850s, at the height of California's golden boom. In these eventful years, mining of a placer variety was carried on deep in the canyons of Monterey's coastal peaks. Much of this early activity is credited to the industrious Chinese, said to have been forced out of their Sierra Nevada claims and who, in wandering the mountains and valleys of Monterey County, had found quantities of both gold and quicksilver.

Reports vary as to when the first hard-rock mining took place, but an 1854 publication on the geology of the coast mountains, by J.B. Trask, states that in addition to placer mining, the mining of gold-bearing rock also took place "to a considerable extent" in the Santa Lucia Range during the summer of 1853.

What results this brief flurry of hard-rock mining produced is unrecorded, but we do have reports of placer mining continuing for many years. One report, from an early Monterey newspaper, tells of $100,000 in gold taken from the Los Burros area of the Santa Lucias in 1869. This report is obviously exaggerated, but serves as proof of continued mining in the area.

By 1875 this same Los Burros area (located in the southwestern section of Monterey County — deep in the heart of the Santa Lucia Mountains) was the scene of such fervent activity that a group of south county pioneers called a miners' meeting and "officially" formed the Los Burros Mining District. The organization meeting was held at the New Year Company's claim on February 5, 1875. Old-time miner, H.C. Dodge, was elected chairman, A.C. Frazier was the choice as secretary, and W.T. Cruikshank was given the distinction of being the first recorder of claims.

The boundaries decided upon at this historic gathering, quoted directly from the original records, are:

> "Commencing at the Mouth of the San Kapoko following the Pacific Ocean Northerly to Premits Trail. Thence following said trail to McKerns. Thence following the Nassimienta to the mouth of the Los Burros Creek. Thence to the place of beginning."

Somewhat confusing to the outsider, the miners of this mountain wilderness knew these boundaries well. Many had spent months and, in some cases, years struggling over the towering peaks and prospecting in the rocky canyons. Finding quantities of gold, silver and copper, these early explorers also found an isolated paradise nestled on the rim of the Pacific.

Other business of importance transacted at this 1875 gathering promised the miners a chance to air their problems. Listed as rule number five, it simply stated ways and means a miner could call for a general meeting. With the cry of "Gold!" in the air, it was ridiculous to assume there would be no problems. Thus, these foresighted miners, many of whom had experienced "gold fever" in camps throughout the state, provided an opportunity for securing mining justice.

For the newly elected recorder of claims, 1875 proved to be a busy year. Aside from his work in the mines, William T. Cruikshank recorded a total of sixty-three claims. Among these early claims were such names as Polar Star, Sea Side, First Chance Quicksilver Mine, Mineral King, Buckeye, Lisbon Quicksilver Mine, and Rough and Ready.

Various other names of interest connected with the Los Burros area in 1875 were: Worlds Pride Vein, Home Stake Lode, Friendship Lode, Calithumpian Quicksilver Lead Lode, Dread Nought Lode, Eureka Gold and Silver Lead Lode, Pacific Quicksilver Ledge and, of course, the not-to-be-forgotten Jenny Lind Lode — obviously named after the popular "Swedish Nightingale" of the mid-1800s.

Continuing through the years, names connected with the Los Burros area have helped to make its history a colorful part of California's past. A sampling of the more imaginative names are: Mud Spring Mine, Lion's Den Ledge (popular with the Chinese), Nip and Tuck Mine, Old Bill Quartz Claim, Scorpion, Lucky Jim Mining Claim, Fighting Chance Mine, Golden Eagle Quartz Claim, Good Boy Placer Claim, Black Mare Claim, Gold Brick Claim, Red Seal Claim, Jack Rabbit Quartz Claim, Yellow Jacket Claim, Stray Dog Quartz Claim, Lovely Water Placer Mine, Good Shooting Placer Claim, T-Bone Quartz Claim, "89" Mine (claimed September 2, 1889), Grizzly Mine, Bravo Mine, Yellow Hammer Quartz Claim, Old Man of the Mountains, Golden Leaf Mine, Hard Luck, Cash Up Quartz Claim, You Bet Mine, Shoo Fly Mine and, to end on a confident note, The Lucky Cuss Mine.

The above list of names is only a minute sampling of the hundreds of place names, mines and claims of the Los Burros Mining District. In the 1880s there were 500 claims in an eight-square-mile area, and an overall listing extends the Los Burros district to more than 2,000 claims. Each name represents its own tiny niche in the area's history, although the Last Chance Mine, the Plaskett Mines, and the long-forgotten community of Manchester played a much larger role in the long and colorful history of this coastal mother lode.

The Last Chance Mine (discovered on March 24, 1887, by William D. "Willie" Cruikshank, son of the recorder of claims) is estimated by the United States Bureau of Mines to have yielded $62,000 in valuable gold ore. One old-timer, born within a stone's throw of the shaft, laughs at this estimate and states, "It was a good deal more that came out of the Last Chance than $62,000!"

Early newspaper accounts also report its productivity to have been considerably higher — with one account listing it at $200,000. The grand old mine eventually succumbed to a flooded shaft, as pumps of the day were not powerful enough to keep an underground spring from sealing its doom. A quote from the book MONTEREY COUNTY, written by E.S. Harrison in the late 1800s and before the shaft flooded, expressed the general feeling of optimism which surrounded this south county bonanza.

"After sinking on the vein several feet, and tracing the ledge to the water edge, three miles away and nearly four thousand feet below, it was resolved to run a tunnel and tap the vein at a depth of more than one hundred feet. This was done, and at a depth of one hundred and forty feet a seven-foot ledge has been encountered, rich as it is, at the surface. To reach it several small veins or stringers were cut through, varying from six to eighteen inches in width. Estimation only on the rock between the lower level and the surface, there are more than $3,000,000 in sight; and if further prospects are not deceptive, this mine will prove one of the richest in California. It is known by the name of Last Chance, and arrangements are now being made to increase the capacity of the mill."

A second quote from the same source predicted an extremely bright future for the Los Burros area: "There is but little doubt that ere this book reaches the East there will be at Los Burros one of the liveliest mining camps in the State."

If it hadn't been for the isolation of the Los Burros area, the backbreaking work required to get the ore out, and the California argonauts' hesitation to chase "another wild goose", strikes like the Last Chance may have proved the above prediction a valid one. As it was, the Los Burros area never really boomed as did so many mining camps of California's famed gold country.

In 1887 the southern portion of Monterey County was sparsely settled — with the cattle population far outnumbering the people. The Spanish ranchos still claimed most of the land, and the once heavily-populated Mission San Antonio (situated in the Los Robles Valley east of the Los Burros area) contained only a fragment of its original population.

Much of the early mining required the ore to be transported over the Pyojo Range of the rugged Santa Lucia Mountains and into the remote Los Robles Valley. The enormity of this task is hard to comprehend unless one is familiar with the Santa Lucia Range. A quote from the "United States Geological Survey Bulletin — 735", in describing Los Burros, helps to portray the inaccessibility of the area. "Travel except on the trails is next to impossible, because of the dense tangle of scrub oak, madrona, and manzanita." A second quote from the same source states, "Cruikshank's discovery at the head of Alder Creek caused only a mild excitement, for the region was rugged, and transportation of supplies and equipment was difficult."

The method preferred by the Cruikshanks in transporting their ore out of the area was slow, costly and troublesome, but proved to be the most feasible of the various methods tried. After the ore had been laboriously removed from the mine's deep shaft, it was broken up and packed in heavy sacks. These sacks were loaded onto the backs of mules, which were led across the Santa Lucia Mountains. Packing the ore as far as the Nacimiento River, the mules were then relieved of their cumbersome burdens. From this point the leader of the pack train (John Harbolt, a one-time Texas Ranger) loaded his weary animals with food, powder, mail and other necessities, and began the long haul back to the mines.

From the Nacimiento River on, the ore was transported by wagon through the small country settlement of Jolon and into the Salinas Valley town of King City. At this point it was transferred to the wonder of the age — the great iron horse, which had only recently reached this valley community. The final lap was over glistening rails to the bay city of San Francisco. Here it was refined into the valuable product that made the whole troublesome process worthwhile.

In later years, the gold-bearing quartz was ground into small chunks by "mule power" (similar to the Mexican arrastra method used in mining camps throughout the state), and still later, the Los Burros area (including the Last Chance Mine) boasted several rock-crushing mills.

Getting the mill's heavy machinery to the Los Burros area presented the miners with a real challenge. Various methods were discussed, with the final solution, judged downright foolhardy by many, calling for a coastal freighter to bring it as far as Cape San Martin, a harbor of sorts on the south county coast. From this jagged outcropping of rock the machinery had to be mounted on sleds and dragged several steep and tortuous miles into the heart of the Los Burros mining territory.

The hard-working mules again proved their worth, as they were dutifully coaxed, pushed, prodded and cursed over the rough Santa Lucia Mountains. With the assorted equipment finally on location, and with the mill's noisy hammers echoing throughout the canyons, the Los Burros Mining District had "come of age".

The small town of Manchester suddenly found itself with a record population of 350 people. A hotel, two general stores, a barber shop, a restaurant, a post office, a blacksmith shop, a one-room school, mess halls, bunkhouses, a number of cabins, a small cemetery, and, of course, a dance hall and a number of saloons made up the town.

Today the town of Manchester is truly a ghost of the past — often referred to as "The Lost City of the Santa Lucias". One old-timer still living in the area accurately commented, "There's nothing left but a field of oats!" He then continued with a tale of how this came to be. "One cold winter night, way back in the nineties, two miners living in a bunkhouse stoked the wood burner a little too full. Before they knew it, things got mighty hot. Not only did the bunkhouse go, but the whole damned town went along with it!"

How Manchester got its name is typical of how gold camps up and down the state were tagged with a brand. As the story goes, "During the early days a huge blacksmith, bearing the name Chester and the strength of a grizzly, got into a scrap with one of the miners. As the fight wore on, Chester's thumb was chawed through in the middle. When Chester realized what had happened to his thumb, he got all the madder and, with one mighty blow, laid the miner out on the hard cold ground!"

13

After the fight a group of spectators were discussing the violent event, and one awed miner commented, "Some man, that Chester!" With that remark the original community of Alder Creek became known as Manchester. (Records indicate that with the coming of the post office on September 14, 1889, the name of Manchester was changed to Mansfield, named after the oldest residents of the area, the Mansfield family of Gorda.)

Other stories give credit to a one-time prospector by the name of Manchester for lending his name to the small Santa Lucia town. History tells us this man was once a captain in the Civil War, and it was he who claimed to have originally interested the Cruikshanks in "hard-rock" mining.

William T. Cruikshank, a native of Troy, New York, had come to California in 1849. He settled in California's famed Calaveras County and didn't venture south until 1872. Not overly interested in mining on his south county holdings, he built a cabin on Villa Creek (in the Los Burros territory) and planted an orchard of apples and plums. Cultivating these, as well as mammoth blackberries raised from cuttings he brought from his Calaveras County home, Cruikshank enjoyed a comparatively quiet life until elected recorder of claims.

Now, a century later, the Cruikshank name is connected with many of the best diggings in the area. William T., with the enthusiastic help of his son William D., are considered by many to be the true mining pioneers of the Los Burros territory.

W.T. and W.D. Cruikshank were alike in many ways while alive, but their stories are even more closely linked in death. In 1907 William (Senior) was hiking out of Los Burros, with plans of visiting far-off San Francisco. He was last seen on the trail leading out of the area. When observed, he appeared to be healthy and making good progress. However, he was never seen again — dead or alive!

Thirty years later, eighty-one-year-old William Cruikshank (Junior) was also hiking out of the Los Burros area. He was making his way toward King City for a holiday gathering at the home of Adrian Harbolt (son of the early mule-train driver and partner of Willie in the prosperous New York Mine). Like his father, Willie never reached his destination. An extensive search was launched, but no trace could be found.

Ten years later, soldiers on maneuvers at Hunter Liggett Military Reservation (which now takes in part of the old Los Burros Mining District) found the bones of a long-dead human. Upon investigation, these remains proved to be those of "young" William Cruikshank. The boots, still strapped to his feet, were identified as belonging to Cruikshank, but even more positive were the remains of a silver watch clasped to his wrist, given to him by his mining partner and bearing the initials of Adrian Harbolt, the man he was on his way to see.

A second family which has played an important role in the history of Los Burros is that of James Krenkel. James Krenkel (Senior), who eventually took William T. Cruikshank's place as recorder of claims, left the historic mining town of Sonora (California) when he heard of the rich Last Chance strike in 1887. Arriving in that eventful year, Krenkel spent the remainder of his life in the Los Burros area.

With Willie Cruikshank, Krenkel worked the Last Chance for a period of time. The mine was eventually sold to the Buclimo Mining Company, with the new owners renaming the mine Buclimo. The name was derived from the combination of stockholders' names: Burnham, Clinton, and Mory. Attempts to work and drain the mine were carried on until near the outbreak of the First World War, when mining costs skyrocketed and expenses became too great to make it pay. Even so, there is evidence that between the years 1912 and 1915 a group from the city of Watsonville (California) invested $75,000 in the development of the mine.

In addition, considerable money was invested by the Buclimo Company on the digging of a 2,100-foot drain tunnel — planned to intersect the Last Chance shaft at a depth of 400 feet. For a time James Krenkel was in charge of digging this tunnel. The breakthrough was looked forward to with great anticipation, but lack of funds stopped the project after 1,860 feet. Cobwebbed steam engines and an old rusted boiler are visible to this day at the entrance to the tunnel — monuments of a bygone era and of a dream that almost came true.

15

After his work in the Last Chance Mine, James Krenkel successfully worked the Oregon Mine for a considerable period of time. While working still another claim, the Gorda Mine, Krenkel found one of the largest nuggets ever to have been taken out of the Los Burros area. This nugget was valued at $1,100 — with gold at that time being worth approximately $20 an ounce. Other nuggets found in the district are said to have been worth more (one nugget found in the Ralston Mine was said to have been cashed in for $1,400, and there is rumor of another having brought $25,000), but old-timers generally agree the Krenkel nugget was the largest to have been taken from Los Burros proper.

In 1901 James Krenkel met his wife-to-be in the small south county community of Pleyto. Before he would marry her he took her "over the mountains" to view the area they would call home. She liked what she saw and they were soon married. The log cabin home of the Krenkels became known throughout Los Burros. Ma Krenkel was affectionately referred to as the "Matriarch of the Mountains", and lived in the district fifty-plus years. She served as nurse to the "people of the peak" and was known as the "official historian" of the Manchester-Los Burros area.

As with most mining areas, the inhabitants of Los Burros had their disagreements. Unfortunately, one set of circumstances led to the death of a member of this pioneer family. Ernest Bauman, known to old-timers as the "Mad Russian", was the principal player in this Los Burros tragedy, with James Krenkel (Junior) being the unlucky victim.

Bauman was said to have jumped ship in San Francisco in 1907. He eventually found his way to the Los Burros area, and in 1913 staked a claim. Reaching a height of only five feet six inches, he weighed a solid 190 pounds. Having massive shoulders, long arms and big hands, Bauman was described in one early newspaper account as walking "with head thrust forward," ambling "over the mountains at a rolling trot like a hurried bear."

He was most often seen wearing a battered hat and dark clothing — with his trusty rifle always by his side. Described by one old-timer, "Bauman was a man of surprising strength and endurance. He would heft two hundred pounds of supplies on his back and trot up the hills like they weren't even there."

In 1937, after quarreling with neighbors and trespassers over mining claims, Bauman began to fight with motorists who used the community road and refused to close his gates. He is said to have fenced his property in hopes of keeping the cattle from the William Randolph Hearst ranch (to the south) from ruining his gardens. On November 8, 1937, after having closed the gate several times, Bauman scattered bent horseshoes and old nails in the ruts of the road.

That night at ten o'clock, a visitor from Berkeley (California) was driving out of the area, and upon passing through Bauman's property the surprised motorist soon found his car had "several" flat tires. Walking to the Krenkel house, he roused Jim Krenkel from bed. With Krenkel and a neighbor, Clarence Webb, the three returned to the stranded automobile. Seeing the roadway sprinkled with an assortment of sharp metal objects, they called for Bauman to "come out and talk!"

From this point on, the details become somewhat clouded. What we do know as fact is that Jim Krenkel was shot in the right breast and died the next day. Ernest Bauman was captured on the tenth of November, walking in a river bed near King City.

An early newspaper account quotes him as saying, "I planted the nails, and shot him with a .35. I aimed high for the breast just like you would kill a deer."

The trial was held early in 1938. After considerable debate, Bauman was acquitted on a plea of self-defense and disappeared from the Los Burros area. In 1954 his bullet-riddled body was found in northern California's Butte County. Accounts say he was killed by an escaped mental patient who was being sought in that area.

Most other violent events have been successfully avoided throughout the years, although a recent discovery near Cape San Martin has brought to light a gruesome tale of violence that many old-timers connect with the history of Los Burros.

This grisly tale first became known in 1962 when four prospectors from the San Francisco Bay Area discovered a mysterious "cave of death!" The century-lost death cave was spotted after bats were observed, seemingly to fly in and out of a Santa Lucia peak.

Discussing the possibility that the bats' tiny cliff-side opening could be the sealed entrance to a larger cave, the gold-seekers wasted little time in working their way up the sloping peak. Finding a tiny aperture in the rock, the eager prospectors settled down to serious digging. After an hour of energetic work they managed to clear an opening large enough for a man to squeeze through.

As the cave opened up, the gruesome sight that greeted the first visitor was one that will long remain etched in his memory. Scattered about the rocky uneven floor were the remains of several long-dead human beings! After the initial shock, he, with the help of his dumbfounded companions, counted the bones of at least ten human skeletons.

Upon exploration, the cave, which initially appeared to contain only one small room, was found to contain several chambers at various depths. Twenty feet inside the entrance, a drop of fifteen feet was discovered. Lowering themselves down the drop, the intrepid explorers found a second drop — taking them approximately fifteen feet deeper into their chamber of horror.

Human skeletons were strewn about on all levels, and the skulls seemed to stare at the men through eyeless holes as they broke the eerie darkness with the beams of their flashlights.

In exploring the lower chamber, additional rooms and tiny passageways were spotted, but large boulders blocked the entrances and they in turn remained uncharted.

Authorities were summoned to the site, and the ghostly find soon was dubbed "Massacre Cave" by the local press. An anthropologist from a leading California institution visited the cave and, after careful examination, tentatively identified all the dead except one as Indians; the other he thought to be of European descent, possibly Spanish.

After examination of the cave by numerous people, including sheriff's deputies and the county coroner, there was general agreement that it had not been lived in by the Indians. There were no signs of smoke on the roof or walls, no artifacts were found, and the rooms or chambers were quite small.

With reports from the anthropologist and the coroner in full agreement, stating that many of the skulls showed signs of having been cracked "as if by a blunt instrument", speculation ran wild as to who could have committed the ancient murders and for what reasons the bodies had been thrown into the cave.

Further reports showed the bones to have been from adults (of both sexes) and that they were between the ages of twenty and forty-five when killed. Evidence also pointed to the deaths as having taken place approximately 100 years before their discovery.

In exploring above the area in which the cave was found, a narrow, spiral-type opening was discovered. A drop of thirty feet to the floor of the death cave gave cause for the majority of onlookers to voice the opinion that the bodies had been tossed into the opening and had fallen to the chambers below.

Knowing the customs of the Indians within whose boundaries the death cave was found, and knowing their tradition of cremating or burying their dead, it became rather obvious that the "entombment" of the bodies was not their accepted practice of preparing members of their own tribe for life in the hereafter.

Possibly a boundary dispute arose and, as occasionally took place, the neighboring tribes did go to war. This simple reasoning, however, does not explain the presence of the lone European.

Another theory discusses the possibility that during construction of Monterey County's scenic coast highway, road workers may have unearthed an aged Indian burial ground. Not wanting to leave the skeletons scattered about, it is thought that these long-ago workers dumped the bones into the spiral-type opening..., letting them come to rest where they fell. Unfortunately, this explanation leaves several questions unanswered, including the existence of the "non-Indian" bones.

here is one story that fits in with many of Massacre Cave's gruesome details, and stems from an early California legend. The tale tells of a group of Indians and a lone soldier who left Mission San Antonio in the early 1800s bound for a small harbor at the mouth of a distant Santa Lucia creek. This creek, known today as Willow Creek, is approximately fifteen miles from Mission San Antonio and is only slightly north of Cape San Martin.

As the story continues, the small party of Indians were heavily burdened with $50,000 in Spanish gold coins destined for a galleon anchored in the Willow Creek harbor. Tellers of this tale claim the party never arrived at its destination and was waylaid by robbers along the way.

Credence to this story comes from several sources, an example being the numerous tales of weekend gold-seekers who claim to have found Spanish coins in the Willow Creek area. One individual even boasted of having found a Spanish gold piece dated 1780! As to where the mission originally obtained such a sizeable fortune appears to be conjecture, with supporters of this theory claiming it was from the sale of Mission San Antonio's prized horses.

The violent deaths the individuals must have experienced, as evidenced from the crushing blows to many of the skulls, also seem to fit in with a possible robbery motive. Unfortunately, after checking the facts, this interesting theory was found to contain several loopholes.

The first of these was that authorities who studied the bones of the dead claimed the subjects had died approximately 100 years before their remains were found, and certainly had not lain in the cave for 150 years. Secondly, there is no known written history from Mission San Antonio telling of the mysterious disappearance of a small band of Indians, or of the disappearance of any money — not to mention $50,000! (As a matter of record, the California missions were not in the habit of collecting large sums of money. They were primarily self-sufficient and usually traded for what little they needed.)

One final note, after checking with a leading authority on California missions, he flatly stated, "I have never heard of any special significance attributed to the horses raised at Mission San Antonio."

Another theory as to what took place on that sloping Pacific peak is directly related to gold in the Santa Lucias. Numerous individuals believe the cave was an early mine, worked by the Indians and discovered by Spanish soldiers. Legends of the mission period tell of one such mine, sometimes called "The Lost Padre Mine", which was stumbled upon by soldiers from the early Spanish stronghold of Monterey.

The captors are said to have forced the Indians into continuing their work in the mine while they pocketed the profits. When the soldiers were finally relieved of their California duties, legend states that they sealed the Indians in the mine hoping to keep its location a secret.

With the known gold activity at neighboring Los Burros, and with Indians known to have worked mines in the area, stories connecting the mysterious death cave to lost gold mines seem to take on added meaning.

Some old-time miners feel that the Indians had found gold and were jumped by eager prospectors. Prospectors, as the history of Los Burros tells us, swarmed the hills approximately 100 years ago. And, as the anthopologist's report tells us, it was approximately 100 years ago that the deaths took place! Possibly this is the answer to the century-old mystery. Perhaps the Indians managed to kill one of their attackers in the long-ago massacre and his body was also thrown into the cave by the "victorious" gold-seekers.

However, other Los Burros veterans feel that it may have been the other way around, pointing out the possibility that the Indians may have waylaid a party of prospectors, hoping to take their gold and avoid the discomfort of having to dig for it themselves. Supporters of this theory suggest that in the ensuing struggle the prospectors got the upper hand and, in turn, did away with their foe.

Whatever the answer to this Santa Lucia mystery may be, numerous theories continue to crop up as the story of Massacre Cave becomes better known. Hopefully, one day a positive clue will be found that will enable historians to piece together the true story of this century-old drama.

A second unsolved mystery of the Los Burros territory also concerns a long-lost cave. Stumbled upon by miner Howard Hilton in the 1950s, this Los Burros legacy has been branded "The Mystery Mine of the Santa Lucias".

With its entrance having long ago been sealed shut, it took considerable time and a great deal of effort to once again open the mine. Upon finally gaining access, Hilton marveled at the hand-carved walls and rounded ceiling as he explored the lengthy shaft.

In discussing his journey into the long-lost mine, Hilton told of seeing miniature stalactites of calcium carbonate and sections of the walls that appeared as white as snow (also from the effects of calcium deposits). He also told of his surprise at the length of the tunnel, which he estimated to be a "whopping" 300 feet!

Descendants of Los Burros pioneers, people whose families hauled gold out of the hills during the boom years, know nothing of the mine, and early records of the Los Burros Mining District shed nary a clue on the mysterious passageway.

As with Massacre Cave, it was not long before speculation arose as to the possibility that this tunnel was the long-sought Lost Padre Mine. However, upon inspection, most old-timers agreed that the corridor of stone showed signs of having been carved during the years of the Los Burros boom, and certainly not one hundred years before (when the Lost Padre Mine was said to have been in existence).

The possibility of its being the fabled Lost Ventana Mine was also discussed, but again it was felt that the tunnel was too recent. Thoughts were also expressed that the cave was too far south to be the Ventana mine, which is said to have been closer to the Big Sur country.

With the mine remaining a Los Burros mystery, it was not long before Hilton made a second discovery — a discovery that added considerable interest to this Santa Lucia corridor of stone.

After giving his find a great deal of thought, and after venturing into the mysterious tunnel a goodly number of times, Hilton began to revise his thinking as to the original purpose of the arrow-straight shaft. With no spurs or exploratory tunnels branching off the main passageway, he began to wonder what it was the parties involved in the long-ago dig hoped to discover at the end of their rainbow.

It was only then that Hilton realized the mystery tunnel was truly headed for a pot of gold! Upon further checking, he backed up his theory with the information that if the tunnel had been continued, it, in all probability, would have intersected the golden vein that had once made the Last Chance the most profitable gold mine in the Santa Lucias!

Aside from mysteries, of which Los Burros has many, a look in depth at this south-coast mother lode reveals the names of numerous pioneer residents (other than the families of Cruikshank and Krenkel) who have played important roles in making Los Burros such a colorful part of California's golden past. Notable among these is the Plaskett family who at one time owned hundreds of acres along California's rugged coast. Leaving their mark by having Plaskett Ridge, Plaskett Rock and Plaskett Creek named after them, this pioneer family literally "rediscovered" the Los Burros area in 1911.

Heading toward home one cold February evening, Lauren and Dudley Plaskett stopped at a creek near the coastal community of Gorda and noticed small flakes of metal resembling gold. They checked more closely and found evidence of an exceedingly rich vein.

Determined not to let this valuable find slip through their fingers, they wasted little time in recording several claims (twenty-three in all). Soon the entire community was buzzing with excitement, and with good reason. A portion of the ore had been sent to San Francisco, with the assay report being highly encouraging.

Word quickly spread of a new south-coast bonanza, with rumors that the Plaskett brothers had turned down an offer of $175,000 for their mine! On May 17, 1911, the Salinas Morning Democrat described a second strike by Dudley Plaskett, and a "sensational" find by "prospector Bushnell". According to the press:

> "The Los Burros mining district in the southern portion of Monterey County has another big wreath to its laurels of fame by the discovery, on Tuesday, May 8th, of what is said by expert miners to be the richest 'find' ever located in that section... The sensational strike made by prospector Bushnell a few days ago in this same section and the Plaskett strike of last Tuesday proves gold mining in Monterey County to be yet in its infancy. The rush of prospectors that will naturally follow these two last big discoveries in this field will bring the Los Burros section back to its old prestige and standing of a few years ago and bids fair to outdo its previous high record, when over six hundred people were maintained by the yellow sands of that vicinity."

The ultimate fate of this promising 1911 Los Burros revival is like retelling the tale of California's famed Mother Lode. The gold gave out..., and with it, the people.

Throughout the long history of the Los Burros Mining District, the name of Melville continues to crop up. The Melville Mine situated on the narrow road leading into Los Burros was founded in the late 1800s, and has been continuously held by this pioneer family ever since. One member, now in his eighties but as spry as most people half his age, laughed heartily when asked how much was taken out of the mine. With a twinkle in his eye he answered, "I don't know how much Dad got, but whenever he needed money he was able to dig out two or three hundred dollars' worth!"

Ed Caldwell, a popular old-time merchant and hotel keeper at Manchester, is said to have dug a well and "found gold in every bucketful of earth he examined." As exaggerated as this may sound, it was duly reported in a Monterey newspaper.

Another early miner, Frank McCormack, always bemoaned the fact he didn't accept an offer of $20,000 for his mine. Years later, after the initial pocket gave out, he sold the mine for a paltry $300.

Paul Acquistapace, who worked the old Brewery Mine (originally discovered in 1888) for thirty-plus years, drove four tunnels through solid rock in his many years of work. This represents an almost unbelievable 2,000 feet of "diggin". With no rich strike to brag about, but refusing to admit defeat, Paul ventured forth each day with renewed hope that it would be his lucky day. Howard Hilton, a close friend of Paul's, philosophically summed up their feelings with his comment, "Mining is like gambling. With the gambler it is always the next roll of the dice or turn of the card. With the miner it is the next lick of the pick."

Few of the old prospectors remain, although numerous claims are still held. Occasionally word of a "rich strike" will spread throughout Monterey County, beckoning modern-day prospectors who, in a brief flurry of excitement, once again bring to life the golden dream of Manchester.

In the late 1940s, two men from King City felt sure they had made such a strike. Quitting their jobs, they moved to Los Burros and eagerly worked their claim. Their rich find, however, only proved to be another prospector's dream, as not enough gold could be taken to make the mine pay.

Again, in the late 1950s, tales of sudden riches spread quickly as two Monterey men claimed to have found a strike "buttered with gold". They had reopened an old shaft (said to have been blasted shut by an angry miner), and were reported to have found ore "assayed at $2,690 worth of gold per ton!" These men invested $5,000 in equipment and set forth to claim a fortune.

Within a year the mine was quiet. These men, as so many others have done in the past, learned that it was much easier to invest in mining equipment than it was to take gold from the ground.

T he year 1970 proved to be a black one in the history of the coastal mother lode. On September 27, nearly a century after the 1875 organization meeting of the Los Burros Mining District, a fire broke out in the rugged Los Padres National Forest. Before the hungry flames were finally brought under control, 45,000 acres were blackened.

In the midst of the desolation lay the Los Burros Mining District. Many of the ancient cabins and miners' shacks that had dotted the canyons and mountain sides were totally destroyed. Aged timbers of long-forgotten tunnels and shafts — mines that had miraculously withstood the ravages of time and countless winter rains — fell to the intense heat and licking flames.

Los Burros veteran Howard Hilton remained at his cabin and fought the fire until two men who feared for his life braved the inferno and dragged him to safety. Hilton compared the scene to that of a snowstorm, "with the flakes being afire!" Charles Krenkel, with the help of Jim Collord (a close friend and neighbor), managed to save the Krenkel cabin, thus preserving a valuable remnant of Los Burros history.

Much of historic value was lost in this south-coast nightmare, but gaping jaws of ancient tunnels, hulking remains of stamp mills, neglected steam engines, and gracefully curving ore bucket tracks are still visible for those who care to look.

Many of the heavily-timbered canyons and forested hillsides were reduced to fire-stripped skeletons rising from ghostly carpets of white ash. With the dense undergrowth of Monterey chaparral virtually eliminated, a surprising number of long-forgotten mines were revealed — mines that had been lost to the Santa Lucia wilderness for countless years. These ancient shafts and forgotten tunnels vividly bring to mind the activity, the dreams, the hopes and the prayers of a bygone generation.

The Los Burros area, surrounded by the Pacific Ocean, Los Padres National Forest and Hunter Liggett Military Reservation, can be reached by way of a narrow, steep and tortuous dirt road. In winter it is impassable except for four-wheel drive vehicles, and even in the summer rugged vehicles are suggested.

The turn-off to this road is unmarked, and lies slightly south of the Cape San Martin warning beacon on California's scenic Highway One. For the hearty explorer of out-of-the-way places, a small picnic area is provided at Alder Creek picnic grounds. But to the uninformed visitor, a word of advice: Honor all "No Trespassing" signs, beware of rattlesnakes, steep cliffs, jagged rocks, poison oak, rusty nails, and — above all — old mines, deep shafts and ancient tunnels. Enjoy what you see, relive a part of California's golden history, and leave the Los Burros Mining District as you found it..., for others to enjoy.

SECTION ONE

The following illustrations are divided into two sections. The first section is composed of old photographs and, in general, shows the Los Burros territory and the surrounding areas as they appeared during the boom years of the Los Burros Mining District. The second section is primarily composed of comparatively recent photographs, many of which show the Los Burros area as it appeared prior to, and just after, the tragic Los Padres National Forest fire of 1970.

PICTURE CREDITS

Allen Knight Maritime Museum Collection (Monterey) — page 60 (top)

Downie (Harry) Collection — page 32 (top)

Harbolt (Adrian) Collection — page 32 (bottom), 33 (top), 34, 40, 41, 50 (top & bottom), 51, 52, 53 & 54

Hathaway (Pat) Collection — page 29 (top & bottom) — C.W.J. Johnson photos & 60 (bottom)

Krenkel (Charles) Collection — page 55

Monterey County Library Collection (Salinas) — page 36, 37, 42 (both), 43, 45, 47, 48 & 56

Monterey History & Art Association Collection — page 30 & 31

Monterey Public Library Collection — page 38 — Max Fisher photo, 39 — Max Fisher photo, 44, 46 — Max Fisher photo, 49 — Max Fisher photo, 57 — Max Fisher photo, 58 — Max Fisher photo & 59 (top & bottom)

Monterey Savings & Loan Collection — page 33 (bottom) & 35 — Max Fisher photo

Mission San Carlos de Borromeo del Rio Carmelo (known today as Carmel Mission) as it appeared about the time of the forming of the Los Burros Mining District — 1875. It was from this church (the second in California's long line of missions) that Padre Junipero Serra's mission Indians are said to have headed south and obtained gold from a hidden mine deep within the Santa Lucias. Many early miners felt this lost bonanza was in the Los Burros area.

The corner of Monterey's busiest intersection (Franklin & Alvarado Streets) as it appeared in 1887, the year of the discovery of the Last Chance Mine. Monterey was the nearest "large" community to the Los Burros Mining District, and was located approximately 55 air miles north of the mining community of Manchester.

The Chinese have played an important part in the history of the Monterey Peninsula as well as in the history of gold in Monterey County. In the 1850s the Chinese were reported to have placer mined in the Jolon and Los Burros areas of Monterey County. Several years later, in 1877 and 1878, reports show the Chinese to have still been at it. In these years, over one hundred Chinese were said to have been at work in the Jolon area, with Messrs. Dutton and Tidball, owners of a Jolon store, having taken in $2,500 in gold dust from these industrious workers. Home to many of these Chinese miners was said to have been the large Chinese settlement located on Monterey Bay's China Point (now called Point Alones — extending to Point Cabrillo, the site of the present-day Hopkins Marine Station). The main street of this picturesque community shows it to be a true "lost treasure" of the Monterey Peninsula.

China Point's Chinese fishing village viewed from the beach. A 1906 fire destroyed this historic landmark. Before the fire, the quaint village was considered the most active settlement of its kind on the Pacific Coast.

Mission San Antonio de Padua as it appeared in 1878. The third in Father Serra's chain of missions, Mission San Antonio was in a sad state of decay during the Los Burros boom. It was from this mission, legend states, that Indians and a lone soldier left for the coast — burdened with $50,000 in Spanish gold coins!

The Dutton Hotel in Jolon as it appeared in the late 1880s. This building was an important meeting place and stage stop in the early days. Known as the Jolon Inn, the building also catered to many of the miners, as Jolon was the jumping-off point for the Los Burros Mining District.

This early hotel in Jolon was also popular with the miners of Los Burros. From the old general store to the left, much in the way of supplies was obtained for the long haul to the mines. The wood frame building is still standing, and today is a landmark of old Jolon.

A pack train to Los Burros as it prepares to leave for the mines from the Ganoung Hotel building shown in the above photo. From Jolon a road led to the Nacimiento River about eight miles away, and from there a trail led through the Santa Lucia wilderness to the mines — a distance of approximately twelve miles.

Packing into Los Burros. The rugged terrain of the Santa Lucias can readily be observed from this early photograph.

Residents of the Santa Lucia community of Manchester gather for a picture. Photo was taken about 1889.

A portion of the main street of "The Lost City of the Santa Lucias". A few of the residents can be seen in this partial view of the mining community.

Manchester's Gem Saloon was a popular meeting place for the people of the Los Burros area. The saloon and general store was owned and operated by Ed Caldwell. Photo was taken about 1889.

A second popular gathering place for the people of Los Burros was the Palace Saloon. As with many mining camps throughout the state, parts of Manchester were hastily constructed and several temporary structures dotted the landscape (as noted by the tent to the right). As described by an old-timer, "The second story of the Palace boasted a lively Manchester hotel." Photo was taken about 1889.

This interior view of a third Manchester saloon shows a bit of "Victorian finery" in the form of gold-leaf mirrors and an ornately decorated backbar. The establishment was known as the Davis Saloon. Unfortunately, the gentlemen are unidentified. Photo was taken about 1889.

John Cruikshank, nephew of William T. Cruikshank, standing in front of "McNeil's Rest". The McNeil home was one of the early buildings in the Los Burros area, and stood until the 1960s when it was destroyed by fire.

A rare photograph of early miners and inhabitants of the Los Burros territory. Unfortunately, the names of these Santa Lucia pioneers were never recorded, and old-timers can identify only two. Sam Pugh, a miner and co-builder of the stamp mill used at the New York Mine, is thought to be the gent in the back row with suit, coat and tie. The man second from right in the front row is said to be Frank McCormack, who turned down an offer of $20,000 for his mine, the King, and later sold it for a meager $300.

William D. Cruikshank, son of William T. Cruikshank, and discoverer of the famed Last Chance Mine.

William T. Cruikshank, elected recorder of claims at the 1875 formation meeting of the newly organized Los Burros Mining District.

The place of discovery. In this canyon is the site of the Last Chance Mine. The cabins shown were the living quarters of the Cruikshanks while working the mine.

To the right, at the base of the scaffolding, is the shaft of the Last Chance Mine — the best paying mine of the Los Burros Mining District. Photo was taken about 1889.

Young Willie Cruikshank stands by the shaft of the Last Chance Mine. It was here that he discovered the gold which led to the hard-rock mining craze of the Los Burros area. Photo was taken about 1889.

The main adit of the Last Chance Mine is said to have intersected the mine shaft at the 97-foot level. The machine in the center is a hand-cranked "blowing machine" which was used to ventilate the mine (rid the mine of smoke after blasting, etc.). The man to the right is said to be Jim Trickle, and James Krenkel is in the center wearing rain-type slicker and hat.

This distant photo, taken at a later date than the previous picture, again shows the main adit of the Last Chance Mine. Ore bucket tracks led to nearby ore bins and a rock-crushing mill.

Shown from a second angle are the the ore bucket tracks which led from the main adit of the Last Chance Mine. As pictured, the tracks are in the process of being laid. When completed they will lead to the site of the ore bins and rock-crushing mill.

One spur of the Last Chance Mine ore bucket tracks led to this somewhat rickety-appearing ramp. From the ramp the ore was dumped down the chute, where it fell to the rock-crushing mill. Tentative identifications state that it is Willie Cruikshank seated on the ramp, and James Krenkel second from right.

Willie Cruikshank's cabin at the New York Mine. The ore bucket tracks led to a nearby stamp mill. Cabin is constructed mostly of redwood shakes. John Harbolt (left), owner of mule train animals and part owner of the New York Mine, and Walter Basham are seen near the cabin.

An assortment of miners, prospectors and visitors to the Los Burros area. Willie Cruikshank's New York Mine cabin is in the background, with (left to right) Walter Basham, David Harbolt (on mule), Jim Trickle, Willie Cruikshank, John Lazier, and John Harbolt in the foreground.

Willie Cruikshank's New York Mine cabin in the foreground, with the mine's blacksmith shop building in the background. John (left) and David Harbolt are standing.

51

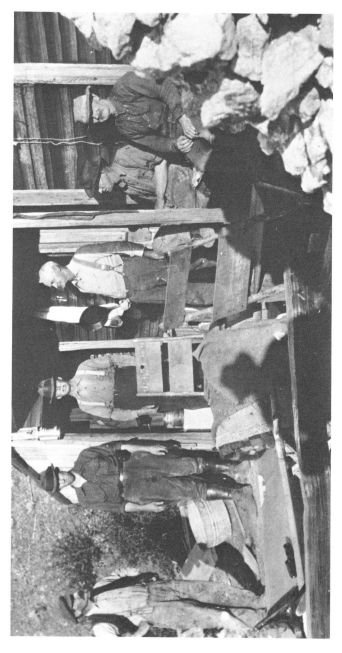

Again we see Jim Trickle, Walter Basham, John Lazier, John Harbolt, David Harbolt and Willie Cruikshank at the New York Mine cabin of Willie Cruikshank. John Harbolt, wielding the frying pan, seems to be daring Trickle to take just one step closer as they ham it up for the camera.

Jim Trickle, John Harbolt, and Willie Cruikshank pose at the entrance to the New York Mine. These three men at one time were partners in the mine, although Willie Cruikshank and Frank McCormack are credited with the discovery. $2,540 is listed as the mine's total profit, but old-timers claim this is only a fraction of the ore it produced.

Willie Cruikshank, founder of the Last Chance Mine and responsible for the Santa Lucia hard-rock mining boom. Willie's appearance somewhat typifies the rugged life lived by the miners of the remote Los Burros Mining District.

James Krenkel, with pick, one of the true mining pioneers of the Los Burros territory. Krenkel arrived in the district in 1887 and remained until he died in 1944. With his wife (affectionately referred to as the "Matriarch of the Mountains") and children, the Krenkel family has added much to the history of Monterey's mother lode. Seen with Krenkel is John Cruikshank, nephew of William T. Cruikshank.

Ma Krenkel (Margaret) flanked by her children and "visiting dignitaries". Left to right (back row) are Charles Krenkel, Hal Krenkel, Ma Krenkel, Doreen Krenkel, Louella Parsons (Deputy County Librarian), the Deputy School Superintendent, and possibly a visiting teacher. In front are Howard and Lillian Krenkel. Bill and Jim, two additional Krenkel children, were not present when the picture was taken.

Other than Cruikshank and Krenkel, the name of Melville has long been connected with the Los Burros Mining District. Above we see the office building of the Melville Mining Company.

Unfortunately, the "Grand Pacific Mine" did not live up to its name. Photo was taken about 1889.

Identified by one old-timer as "possibly" the Cool Spring Mine. Photo was taken about 1889.

Much has been said about the Brewery Mine, which was founded in 1888. It was this mine that Paul Acquistapace spent over 30 years of his life working. Perhaps Paul's persistence was spurred on by the $11,000 that is "rumored" to have been taken from the mine during its early years of existence.

Coastal freighter GIPSY. The usual run for this ship of the Pacific Coast Steamship Company was San Francisco, Santa Cruz, Moss Landing, Monterey, and San Simeon. The small freighter also made stops in between, and is thought to be the ship that carried the heavy stamp mill equipment to the south county "port" of Cape San Martin. The GIPSY as seen in this picture is shown leaving Monterey Bay in 1901.

Unfortunately, the proud little GIPSY met her end on Monterey's Macabee Beach (where world-famed Cannery Row now stands) in September of 1905.

SECTION TWO

A surprising number of mining-day memories could be seen throughout the Los Burros Mining District prior to the disastrous Los Padres National Forest fire of 1970. The following photographs, in most instances, show the area, as well as many of the mining-day relics as they appeared before and after the 1970 fire.

PICTURE CREDITS

Crisan (John L., Jr.) Photos & Collection — page 64 & 65

Harbolt (Adrian) Collection — page 70 (full photo)

Leaman (Myrtle) Collection — page 66 (bottom) & 70 (inset)

Monterey Peninsula Herald Collection — page 101 (top & bottom) & 102 (top) — Ben Lyon photos

Reinstedt (Randall A.) Photos & Collection — page 63 (top & bottom), 66 (top), 67 (top & bottom), 68, 69 (top & bottom), 71 (top & bottom), 72, 73, 74 (top & bottom), 75 (top & bottom), 76 (top & bottom), 77 (top & bottom), 78, 79, 80, 81 (both), 82 (top & bottom), 83 (top & bottom), 84, 85 (top & bottom), 86, 87, 88, 89 (top & bottom), 90 (top & bottom), 91 (top & bottom), 92, 93 (top & bottom), 94 (top & bottom), 95 (top & bottom), 96 (top & bottom), 97 (both), 98 (top & bottom), 99 (top & bottom), 100, 102 (bottom) & 103

Every effort has been made to credit photos accurately. If mistakes are found, please notify **GHOST TOWN PUBLICATIONS** (address on page two), and corrections will be made on subsequent printings.

The entrance to the Los Burros district as it appears from California's scenic Highway One. A turn to the left after crossing the cattle guard and a rugged seven-mile drive over a steep and tortuous rut-filled road brings one to the heart of the Los Burros Mining District.

Cape San Martin looking south. A portion of California's Highway One is visible to the left. It is slightly south of this point that the Los Burros turnoff is located. This south county point also marks the spot where the cumbersome stamp mill equipment was brought by ship. Slightly north of this point is the outlet of Willow Creek and the site of Monterey County's mysterious Massacre Cave.

A small collection of bones brought from various depths of Massacre Cave are seen at the entrance to this Santa Lucia death cave.

A grisly display of four of the skulls taken from Massacre Cave. The skull at left is believed to be the only "non-Indian" skull of the ten that were recovered. The large bone at the bottom of the picture is said to be nonhuman and is thought by many to have been a weapon used in the long-ago massacre.

While passing through the Los Padres National Forest and on into the Los Burros area, a small stream must be forded, and extreme caution must be taken in negotiating hairpin turns and watching for animals that are frequently seen along the narrow road.

Construction of the Los Burros road in the early 1930s. To the left of the aged Caterpillar tractor, five Los Burros veterans who helped with the road construction pose in front of their vintage automobile. George Artley is the man in the center. The man to Artley's left is tentatively identified as Reuben Pugh, and the man to his right is thought to be Edwin Harriss. The men on each end are unidentified.

As one neared the heart of Los Burros (before the 1970 fire) he passed the old Melville home. As was the case with most of the early buildings, it was shaked and was not of elaborate proportions.

The Melville home survived the fire that destroyed the town of Manchester, but this was the scene of the rustic cabin after the fire of 1970.

67

The Melville barn as it appeared before the 1970 holocaust.

Tucked neatly behind the barn was the all-important outbuilding — a symbol of a bygone era.

Mining-day relics found in the ashes of the Melville barn.

69

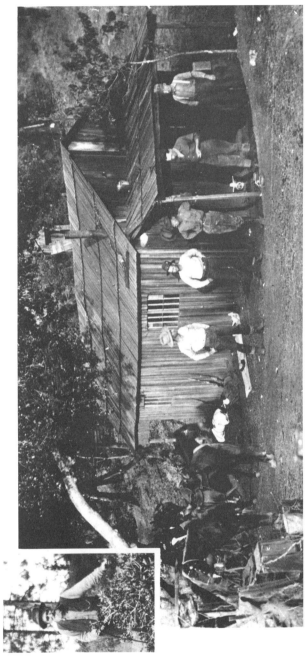

A story only pictures can tell. The original photo (above) is said to have been taken in the late 1800s. The cabin was owned by Sam Pugh (inset), a well-known prospector and miner of the Los Burros area. The second photo (top — opposite page), taken from approximately the same angle as the original photo, shows the cabin with well over three-quarters of a century of weathering behind it (taken approximately one month before the 1970 fire). The last picture (bottom — opposite page), also from the same angle, was taken a few days after the 1970 fire, and graphically illustrates what a careless camper can do to a historic structure.

The entrance to the once active and profitable Blue Jay Mine (also known as the Manchester Mine), before the 1970 fire. The licking flames destroyed the wood supports, causing a portion of the entrance to collapse.

The above photo, and those that appear on the following three pages, offer different views of the ancient stamp mill of the once-prosperous Blue Jay Mine as it appeared before and after the 1970 Los Burros fire. Before the fire the steam engine and actual workings of the machinery appeared to be in remarkably good condition, considering the length of time they had been exposed to the elements. Aside from a little rust, a vast network of cobwebs, dried leaves and grass, and a few fallen timbers, the old five-stamp mill appeared to have survived her years of neglect relatively unscathed. After the 1970 Los Burros nightmare, all that was left to greet visitors were blackened remains of iron and steel.

Before and after scenes of the Blue Jay Mine stamp mill. See page 73 for complete caption.

Before and after scenes of the Blue Jay Mine stamp mill. See page 73 for complete caption.

Before and after scenes of the Blue Jay Mine stamp mill. See page 73 for complete caption.

Looking like a small tool shed from the outside, the sign on the door gives away the secret of what one will find on the inside. Howard Hilton's Lucky Mo Mine survived the 1970 fire, and should have another warning added to the "Danger" sign — as this is a favorite "hangout" of deadly rattlesnakes.

Inside the shack, the Lucky Mo Mine represents a staggering amount of work as seemingly endless ore tracks lead to a dark underground world.

77

A mystery of the Los Burros Mining District was presented to the old-timers of the area in the late 1950s. In these eventful years Howard Hilton discovered what is known today as "The Mystery Mine of the Santa Lucias". Rumors that the long-lost mine was the Ventana Mine or the Lost Padre Mine immediately arose; but they were soon discounted, as there is general agreement that the tunnel was dug during the Los Burros boom (much later than the Lost Padre Mine and the Ventana Mine are thought to have been worked). To add to the mystery, the arrow-straight passageway was found to be headed straight for the golden vein of the Last Chance Mine — located on the opposite side of the hill!

Hand-carved walls and a rounded ceiling can readily be observed in this interior view of "The Mystery Mine of the Santa Lucias".

One of the numerous tunnels that dot the Los Burros area. Today, tunnels such as this are little more than nameless ghosts that gape auspiciously at the visitor who wanders the canyons and hillsides of the Los Burros Mining District. With the 1970 fire burning much of the underbrush, many tunnels and shafts that were once lost to the Santa Lucia wilderness have since come to light.

The visitor to the Last Chance Mine's main adit once had to fight through a forest of poison oak, and delicately sidestep the prickly offerings of cactus, if he wished to get a close view of this ancient tunnel. After the 1970 fire, the once-hidden adit was considerably easier to reach.

Less than fifty yards from the road, and falling over four hundred feet straight down, was the main shaft of the Last Chance Mine. Begun in the late 1880s, this water-filled shaft represented a staggering amount of work, and was considered one of the danger spots of the district.

The results of the fire's hungry flames can readily be seen in this photo. The destruction of timbers and shored-up walls made the shaft of even greater danger to visitors.

Part of the original equipment used at the Last Chance shaft — prior to the 1970 fire.

The same corrugated shed — after the fire.

Above and on the next page are a variety of views of the cobweb-covered and slightly rusted remains of steam engines and boilers used in the digging of the Buclimo Mining Company's 1,860-foot drain tunnel. This tunnel was planned to intersect the main shaft of the Last Chance Mine, and when work was stopped, the tunnel was less than three-hundred feet from the shaft. As with many of the remaining relics of the Los Burros area, the district's 3,000-foot elevation, combined with the many mountain ridges between it and the distant Pacific, has left these ghosts of yesteryear relatively untouched by the damaging effect of salt air. Considering the effects of the fire, together with their age and lack of care, the relics are in remarkably good condition and provide the visitor with an excellent view of Los Burros as it once was.

85

In this view of the machinery used in digging the Buclimo Mining Company's 1,860-foot drain tunnel, the entrance to the Los Burros "tunnel of tunnels" can be seen.

A second view of the 1,860-foot drain tunnel reveals a small sign above the entrance with the following strongly-worded message:
BUCLIMO MINING COMP.
PRIVATE PROPERTY
DANGER
NO TRESPASSING

After the fire the remarkable drain tunnel presented an entirely different picture.

Ore bins of the Last Chance Mine, before the 1970 fire. The bins were approximately three stories high and were last used in the 1930s.

All that remained of the ore bins, after the fire.

Corrugated metal shed that originally stood next to the ore bins of the Last Chance Mine, before the 1970 fire.

Remains of the corrugated shed, after the fire.

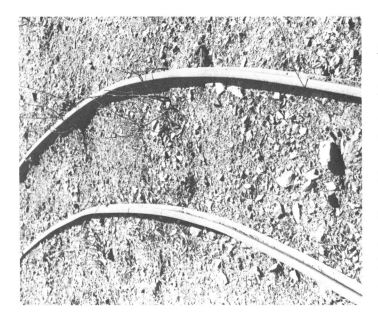

Ore bucket tracks (before and after the fire) still lead from the main adit of the Last Chance Mine to the site of the ore bins.

There is reported to be a network of over 1,000 feet of tunnels, shafts and drifts within this constricted entrance to the Grizzly Mine. The Grizzly Mining Company (founded in 1889) had as its superintendent H.C. Dodge, the first president of the Los Burros Mining District. In the early days the mine's ore was crushed by the arrastra method powered by water from nearby Alder Creek. This method was abandoned in the late 1890s, and a two-stamp mill was erected to take its place. This claim was eventually purchased by the Buclimo Mining Company. In the years 1890, 1902, 1903 and 1904, the Grizzly Mine is recorded as having yielded $9,515 in gold and $33 in silver. The pictures on the following three pages show the Grizzly Mining Company's two-stamp mill — before and after the 1970 Los Burros fire.

Grizzly Mine stamp mill. See page 92 for complete caption.

Grizzly Mine stamp mill. See page 92 for complete caption.

The "field of oats" where once stood the bustling mining community of Manchester.

After the 1970 fire the site of Manchester was once again an ash-covered flat.

Partial remains of the small cemetary near the once-thriving community of Manchester. This neglected grave is that of Fred Tomlinson who died on December 4, 1909. Cause of death is reported to have been due to a fall down a mine shaft.

Relics of bygone days are to be found throughout the Los Burros district. On these two pages we see an old Wedgewood stove, the remains of a once-powerful steam engine and its accompanying boiler, part of a discarded ore bucket car, and "wheels" from an abandoned stamp mill.

The rusted and bullet-pierced remains of what appears to be an early Ford are also a part of the Los Burros landscape.

Then came the fire! A smoke-filled Santa Lucia canyon with fingers of flame racing up the hillside.

A forested hillside almost lost from view in the dense smoke of the Los Padres National Forest fire.

Caught in the inferno, a citizen of the Santa Lucias (commonly referred to as a tarantula) heads for safety and away from the heat and flames that destroyed his home.

Once green and inviting, the Los Burros district took on a ghostly air after the devastating fire.

A grim reminder of the 1970 holocaust is represented by this fire-singed sign — hanging in the middle of the fire-ravaged Los Burros area — reminding all visitors not to smoke!

A FINAL THOUGHT...

With the price of gold rising to dizzying heights, as compared to an approximate $20 an ounce, as was the case when Los Burros boomed, one can't help but wonder how the "golden history" of MONTEREY'S MOTHER LODE would have differed if the Los Burros Mining District had been formed in 1975..., rather than one century before...